Climate Change
Heatwaves *and* Big Freezes

Contents

Written by Mio Debnam

Collins

T0321639

1 What is global warming?

Did you know there have been five ice ages in the last two billion years? In between them, Earth's temperature has changed slowly, from hot to cold and back again in cycles.

This was caused by tiny differences in Earth's path around the Sun, and volcanic activity – which changed how much sunshine reached Earth's surface and how much heat could be trapped in the **atmosphere**.

But, around 10,000 years ago, volcanic activity slowed, causing Earth's temperature to **stabilise**. It's hardly changed since! This has allowed all living things, including humans, to thrive.

In the last 50 years, however, temperatures have crept upward. This is global warming. In 2015, Earth's "average temperature" was the hottest it's been in 11,000 years!

So, how much hotter is it? Earth's average temperature has risen 1.2 degrees Celsius in the last 120 years.

You're probably thinking, "that's not much!" – and you're right. If your bath water was 1.2 degrees Celsius warmer today than yesterday, you'd barely notice. But even that small rise is causing **climate** change and extreme weather.

Rising temperatures cause heatwaves and dries up the water in rivers and in the soil, causing **drought**.

Heatwaves can also disturb the winds that blow around the world – so that winds that usually bring rain to a region no longer do so, or cause the icy winds that normally stay above the North and South Poles to shift and take freezing weather to unexpected places.

Higher temperatures and warmer oceans also make larger storm clouds form over the ocean, resulting in huge hurricanes.

Scientists are concerned because temperatures are still rising. They warn that if we do nothing, the average annual temperature may rise by four degrees Celsius by 2100!

Think about it

How do you think rising temperatures will affect life on Earth?

2 Unbalanced ecosystems

Ecosystems support tens of thousands of different living things – plants, animals and tiny life forms, such as bacteria. Some, like plants, make food. Others eat the plants and are themselves eaten. This is called a food chain.

Climate change unbalances ecosystems.

For example: In a rainforest ecosystem, insects thrive and their numbers increase as temperatures rise. But if their numbers grow a lot, they may eat so much that they kill the plants they need for food, then die off themselves. Then insect-eating birds would leave, and predators, like ocelots, that feed on birds would go hungry, and so on.

Each change causes another. If enough changes occur, entire ecosystems can break down.

Think about it

What would happen if all the lions disappeared from an African grassland ecosystem?

an ocelot hunting (Amazon rainforest)

3 In the countryside

If you're living in a **temperate** climate like the UK, you're probably enjoying some effects of global warming. Winters are milder, and daffodils, which used to bloom in March, flower as early as January!

Many farmers are happy with the longer spring and summer season, as they can grow more crops.

But, what else do you think climate change affects?

It affects rainfall – causing heavier rainfall in winter in the UK, leading to floods.

There's also less rain in summer, which is great for picnics, but terrible for plants and animals, as their water supply shrinks.

Focus on frogs

Frogs need water to live and breed. But the hotter, drier summers caused by climate change have made some ponds and streams dry up. It's also helped increase the spread of a frog-killing virus. By 2100, the "*croak*" of frogs in Britain may become a rare sound, as some frog **species** are facing **extinction**.

frog with frogspawn (UK)

Climate change also affects birds. The number of robins is increasing as they're more likely to survive a warmer winter. Things aren't so good for European cuckoos.

Cuckoos spend the British winters in Central Africa before **migrating** 5,000 kilometres to the UK in April, to breed.

They don't build nests. Instead, they lay their eggs in the nests of another (much smaller) bird, then leave, relying on the **host** to look after the cuckoo chick.

In the past, cuckoos could lay their eggs when the host did. But now that it's warmer, the supply of insects the chicks need for food is plentiful earlier. This means the host birds can nest earlier.

By the time cuckoos reach the UK, host birds have finished raising their young and have left, so the cuckoo population is now a third of what it was 25 years ago.

host feeding a cuckoo chick (UK)

4 High in the mountains

Even in summer, it can be freezing cold on mountaintops.

Pikas are small animals related to rabbits. They live on mountain peaks.

During the short warm season, they scurry around all day gathering grass.
They use the grass to build a "haystack" which dries in the sun, so they'll have food for the nine months of snowy weather.

You'd think that warmer summers would help, but their coats are so thick that if temperatures rise to 25 degrees Celsius for more than a few hours, pikas can overheat and die.

How about milder winters?

They're no good either. Pikas need deep snow to build snow burrows that protect them from predators and extreme cold!

a pika building its haystack (USA)

Think about it

How are the pikas' snow burrows similar to igloos?

13

Many mountain creatures, such as arctic foxes, snowshoe hares, stoats, and birds called ptarmigans, are brown during summer. This helps them "blend in" with the trees, earth and rocks.

But in autumn, as the hours of sunlight become fewer, their bodies react by swapping their brown fur or feathers, with a white replacement.

This helps **camouflage** them, so they can't be spotted in a snowy environment. But what if there's no snow?

snowshoe hare, winter

arctic fox, winter

The shorter snowy season is bad news for white hares and ptarmigans as they're more likely to be caught by a hungry bear. It also makes it harder for white-coated predators like the stoat and fox to sneak up on their prey.

Snowshoe hares and arctic foxes from Greenland are well camouflaged in summer, but in winter they need snow to blend in.

snowshoe hare, summer

arctic fox, summer

5 On the climate change escalator

With temperatures rising, around half of the animal and plant species on Earth have started moving!

Global warming has benefitted hot weather lovers like mosquitos and Burmese pythons. They've spread to areas that were once too cold.

However, species not suited to warmer weather have been escaping the heat by moving towards the Poles, or to higher ground, where it's cooler.

But what happens to them when the mountain peaks become too crowded, or even worse, too warm?

Once they reach the top, they have nowhere else to go, and may die out. Scientists call this upward migration "the escalator to extinction".

Apollo butterfly

6 The shrinking ice!

Did you know the South Pole is on a frozen land (called Antarctica) surrounded by sea ice, but at the North Pole, there's just sea ice floating on the Arctic sea?

Some sea ice is three to seven metres thick and has been frozen for more than four years. Annual sea ice forms and melts yearly – it's approximately 30 centimetres thick.

In the past, the amount of ice that froze in winter and melted in summer was the same, but now, more ice melts in summer than refreezes in winter.

The Arctic and Antarctic are warming twice as fast as anywhere else on Earth. In 20 to 30 years, the Arctic may be ice-free in summer.

Ships will be able to travel easily across areas that used to be frozen solid. But it's not great for Earth's climate – can you guess why?

White sea ice reflects sunshine and heat back upwards. But when it melts, the dark seawater absorbs heat, making the ocean even warmer.

Rising temperatures also melt the massive ice sheets covering the land in Antarctica.

When land ice (ice sheets, glaciers and mountain snowcaps worldwide) melts, this "new" water flows into the ocean, making sea levels rise.

If nothing changes, by 2100, sea levels will rise a further 30 to 50 centimetres. Scientists think that if global warming speeds up, it may rise as much as 250 centimetres! This would cause coastal flooding and many more hurricanes – a good reason to try to control global warming.

Experiment

Half fill two tall glasses marked "A" and "B" with water. Float three ice cubes in glass A to represent floating sea ice. Put three ice cubes in a separate bowl – this represents ice sheets on Antarctic land. Mark the water levels in each glass with rubber bands.

Leave the ice to melt. Pour the water in the bowl into glass B.

Check the water levels.

The water level in A shouldn't change, because floating ice (sea ice and icebergs) takes up the same space as the water does, when it melts. The level in B should rise – like sea levels rise when ice sheets melt.

Emperor penguins need strong sea ice to raise chicks on (Antarctica)

7 In the Arctic ecosystem

Female polar bears give birth in December and stay with the cubs until they're ready to leave their snow den. Mothers feed their cubs milk, but don't eat themselves. By the time they leave their dens in April, mother bears are thin and hungry.

Polar bears mostly hunt on sea ice. They wait next to **breathing holes**, grabbing seals when they come up for air. It's easier than catching a seal in open water.

The mother catches about two-thirds of the food that she and her cubs need for the whole year in the few weeks before the ice melts.

Recently, many bears have gone hungry and been unable to raise cubs. The ice melting earlier in spring and forming later in autumn has reduced their hunting time.

polar bear with cub (Norway)

Although polar bears are strong swimmers, they need sea ice to rest on. It's particularly important for the cubs if they have to swim long distances with their mother in search of food.

Arctic seals give birth to, and raise their pups, on sea ice too. Harp and ringed seal pups can't swim for the first few weeks. They must stay on the ice, until their mother's rich milk fattens them up and they grow waterproof fur, so they won't freeze in the icy water!

harp seal and pup at a breathing hole (Canada)

The pups develop quickly, but if the ice breaks up before they're old enough to swim long distances and catch fish, they can't survive.

Arctic sea ice contains no soil, so no trees or grass grow there. But peer underneath, and you'll find a thick carpet of sea ice algae growing.

Algae is a plant-like living thing, that uses sunlight and **nutrients** to make food.

It's a rich source of food for tiny creatures such as krill, which are eaten by many **marine** animals, like fish, squid, clams, and even whales.

The smaller creatures are eaten by bigger fish, seals, whales and birds, which in turn are hunted by polar bears.

Think about it

If the ice melts early, the ice algae has nowhere to grow. How do you think this will impact the Arctic food chain?

krill feeding on sea ice algae

8 In warmer waters

Earth is called "The Blue Planet" because more than two thirds of it is covered by ocean.

Only a small amount of ocean is coastal (close to land), but huge numbers of marine plants and animals live there.

Coastal waters are shallow enough to let sunlight reach algae. These waters are also rich with nutrients washed into the ocean from land. The sunshine and nutrients allow the algae – tiny floating phytoplankton, seaweeds and in corals – to grow and make food.

The algae attracts lots of animals. **Kelp** forests and coral reefs are two of the busiest and most **diverse** ecosystems in the world. They're sometimes called "the rainforests of the sea"!

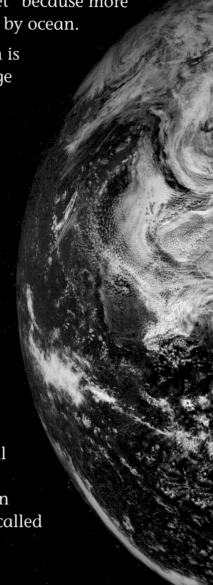

Earth, from space

Kelp and coral need cool water to thrive. The rising ocean temperature has resulted in the loss of many kelp forests and has caused half of the world's coral reefs to **bleach** and die.

There's also another problem.

Gases, such as oxygen, dissolve naturally in water. Fish don't have lungs like us, but they need oxygen to live. Luckily, they have gills that allow them to use the oxygen in the water.

Unfortunately, **carbon dioxide** also dissolves in water. High levels of carbon dioxide in the air, caused by humans burning **fossil fuels**, is a problem, because when too much dissolves, it makes the ocean too acidic.

Coral reefs support thousands of species.

This affects animals such as clams and crabs, and also corals, as the acid dissolves their shells and hard outer skeletons, so they can't grow!

Marine animals need coral reefs and kelp forests for shelter and food. When these **habitats** are destroyed, the entire ocean ecosystem suffers, reducing the number of living things it can support.

bleached coral

Think about it

What would happen to fish if oxygen didn't dissolve in water?

Climate change also affects marine turtles, for an unexpected reason.

Female turtles dig holes on beaches and then bury their eggs in the sand, before leaving.

Surprisingly, whether the eggs develop into males or females depends on the temperature!

If the sand is between 27.5 to 31 degrees Celsius, a mixture of male and female babies will develop. When global warming makes the sand too warm, mostly females are born.

In time, this lack of male turtles will lead to extinction.

Think about it

What would happen if
the sand temperature stayed
below 25 degrees Celsius
for decades?

green turtle burying eggs, India

9 Burning forests and bushlands

Trees not only absorb carbon dioxide from the air, they draw up water from the soil and release it into the air. This helps the formation of clouds and rain around a rainforest region.

When we cut down trees, a cycle starts. Fewer trees equals less rain, which, with rising temperatures, dries the forest. Higher temperatures cause more lightning to form. When struck by lightning, dry trees burn easily, so there are fewer trees. Burning wood releases carbon dioxide, which traps heat, making it even hotter!

Due to recent scorching summers, there's been a rise in forest and bushfires in areas such as California (USA), Australia, Indonesia, Brazil, Angola, South Africa and Siberia (Russia).

When a forest dies, the unprotected soil becomes dry and unable to support plant and animal life. The ecosystem collapses and the area may become desert, as it has in parts of Africa and India.

Orangutans are facing extinction as rainforests disappear. (Borneo)

10 How we affect climate and how climate affects us

In the last 120 years, the human population has grown five times larger. To house and feed everyone, many forests have been cut down to build more factories, farms and cities. Billions of humans working, playing and travelling has resulted in more fossil fuels being burnt than ever before.

As a result, we've produced so much carbon dioxide that levels are the highest they've been in 800,000 years!

We also produce another gas called methane, from farming – particularly from cows, which burp methane.

These "greenhouse gases" occur naturally too – which is good, because without them Earth would be frozen and lifeless! But current levels are trapping too much heat in our atmosphere.

Climate change causes extreme and sometimes surprising weather – both heatwaves and deep freezes!

Heatwaves don't just dry up streams and lakes, they cause less snow to fall on mountaintops than before. Two billion humans worldwide depend on snow melting in the mountains and running downhill, for their water supply during the hotter, drier summer months. They're now facing water shortages.

Athens, Greece, covered in snow

Elsewhere, climate change has disrupted the winds that travel around the world, so they now sometimes carry frosty polar air to unexpected places! Because of this, in recent years, Texas (USA), Madrid (Spain) and Athens (Greece), all known for mild winters, have been hit by freezing storms that covered the cities with snow.

Think about it

Ask some adults how weather patterns have changed since they were young.

11 All is not lost!

Climate change seems like such a huge problem that it's hard to see how individuals can make a difference.

We need governments to make changes. For example, they could develop and use more clean, **sustainable** energy sources, replant native forests and protect diverse species.

But… there are things we should do to help too.

By changing our behaviour, we can all reduce the amount of greenhouse gas that we produce.

It may not seem like much, but if we all do a little, together we can do a lot to stop climate change from getting worse!

What should we do?

12 Suggestions for change

You don't need to do everything, but every little counts.

Belongings

Factories burn fuel to make new things so:

Use what you have a bit longer.

Reuse and recycle.

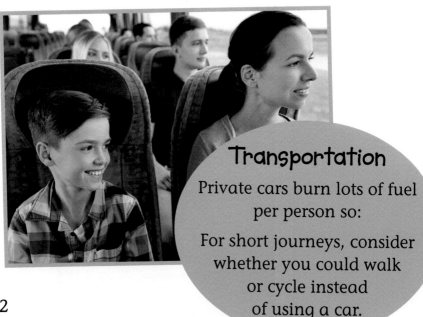

Transportation

Private cars burn lots of fuel per person so:

For short journeys, consider whether you could walk or cycle instead of using a car.

Electricity

Creating power releases pollution into the air, so:

Shut windows/doors so heated/cooled air can't escape.

Turn off TVs, computers, lights, and so on, when not using.

Take shorter showers.

Food

Farming, especially raising animals, uses fuel and water and produces lots of methane so:

Make sure you don't waste food!

Learn

Climate change is complicated. It's affected by, and affects, many things.

Learn what you can. Perhaps, one day, you'll become a leader for change!

Glossary

atmosphere layer of air surrounding Earth

bleach turn white

breathing holes holes in sea ice used by seals, to breathe

camouflage blend in with the surroundings

carbon dioxide gas that most animals breathe out; also produced by burning fuel

climate typical weather patterns of a place

diverse with many different types

drought extended period without enough rain

ecosystems groups of living things interacting with each other and the environment

extinction when the last of the species dies

fossil fuels oil, gas, coal, and so on

habitats the natural homes of living things

host owner of the nest

kelp large brown seaweed

marine of the sea

migrating moving from one place to another

nutrients parts of food which keep the body healthy

species group of similar living things

stabilise to stop changing

sustainable will never run out

temperate climate with four seasons; no extreme temperatures

Index

Climate change around the world

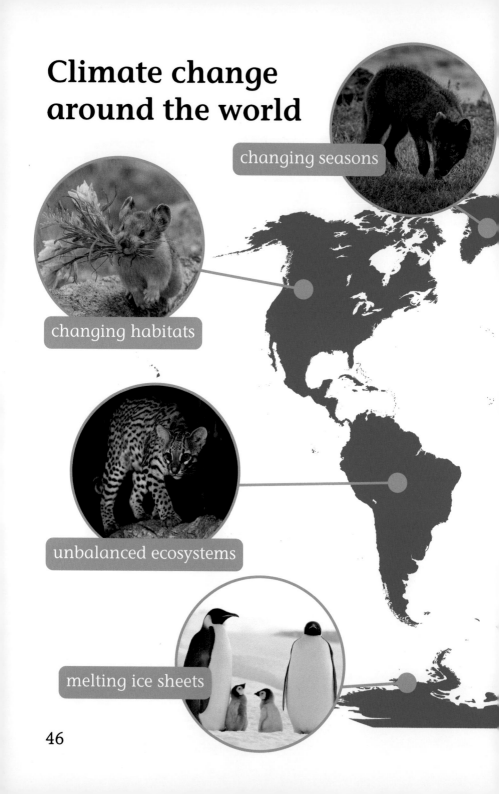

changing seasons

changing habitats

unbalanced ecosystems

melting ice sheets

changing animal behaviour and population

forest fires

bleaching coral reefs

Ideas for reading

Written by Christine Whitney
Primary Literacy Consultant

Reading objectives:
- be introduced to non-fiction books that are structured in different ways
- listen to, discuss and express views about non-fiction
- retrieve and record information from non-fiction
- discuss and clarify the meanings of words

Spoken language objectives:
- participate in discussion
- speculate, hypothesise, imagine and explore ideas through talk
- ask relevant questions

Curriculum links: Science: Living things and their habitats; Writing: Write for different purposes

Word count: 3079

Interest words: climate, global warming, ecosystem, habitats, sustainable

Resources: paper, pencils and crayons, access to the internet

Build a context for reading

- Ask children to share their memories of the hottest and coldest places they have experienced.

- Look closely at the title and front cover of the book. Ask the group to discuss each image in relation to the title. How are they connected?

- Read the blurb and ask children to share what they already know about *climate change*. Ask what they expect to find out about in this book.

Understand and apply reading strategies

- Read together up to the end of Chapter 1. Ask children to complete this sentence – *Global warming is ...*

- Continue to read to the end of Chapter 2. Challenge children to explain what an *ecosystem* is and how *climate change* can *unbalance* one.

- Read on to the end of Chapter 3. Ask children to give examples of how *climate change* is having an effect in countries with a temperate climate, like the UK.

- In Chapter 4, page 15, it says, *The shorter snowy season is bad news for white hares and ptarmigans.* Ask for a volunteer to explain why this is so.